FACT OR FICTION

D0634812

ALIENS, MONSTERS AND GHOSTS

Jim Pipe

ticktock

FACT OR FICTION?

ALIENS, MONSTERS AND GHOSTS

Copyright © ticktock Entertainment Ltd 2007

First published in Great Britain in 2007 by ticktock Media Ltd,
2 Orchard Business Centre, North Farm Road, Tunbridge Wells, Kent, TN2 3XF

ticktock project editor: Jo Hanks
ticktock project designer: Sara Greasley
With thanks to: Sally Morgan and Elizabeth Wiggans

ISBN 978 1 84696 674 3 pbk

Printed in China

Picture credits (t=top; b=bottom; c=centre; l=left; r=right):
Mehmet Alci: 70bl. Amit Gogia CyberMedia Services: 26/27 (main pic), 90/91 (main pic). Mark Bond: 8tl. Linda Bucklin: 36/37 (main pic). Marina Cano Trueba: 62/63. Corbis: 9 (main pic), 50/51 (main pic). CVP: 80/81 (main pic). Christian Darkin: 60bl. Nathan B Dappen: 92/93 (main pic). Gilles DeCruyenaere: 64/65, 70/71 (main pic). Denisenko: 66bl. Domhnall Dods: 52/53 (main pic). electricsoda: 12bc, 12br. Mary Evans Picture Library: 22bl. Fortean Picture Library: 14bl, 2b, 65, 71, 72bc. Rudolf Georg: 58tl. Getty: 32cl, 39 (main pic), 48/49 (main pic). Johanna Goodyear: 13cl. Chris Harvey: 10/11 (main pic: hands), 68/69 (main pic), 80tl. Alan C. Heison: 15 (main pic). Craig Hosterman: 76cb. Image Select: 92tl. Stephen Inglis: 24bc. Barbara Jablonska: 93tr. Ritu Manoj Jethani: 60/61 (main pic). Milos Jokic: 56/57 (main pic: chicken). Adrian T Jones: 48bl. Sarah Johnson: 68cb. Pam Kane: 84tl. Raymond Kasprzak: 81bl. Roman Krochuk: 31bl. Evgeny E. Kuklev: 13cr. LEACH: 36bl. Jimmy Lee: 86bl. Emily H Locklear: 56bl. Patricia Malina: 76tl. Mark: 62tl. Michael Marquand: 88tl. NASA Picture Library: 32/33 (main pic), 33tl. Kevin Norris: 85tl. Tyler Olsen: 22/23 (main pic). C. Paramount/Universal/Everrett/Rex Features OFC: 38tl, 54/55, 58/59, 67cr. Vladimír Radosa: 74/75 (main pic). Styve Reineck: 24/25 (main pic). Science Photo Library: 18-19 (main pic), 21br. ShutterStock: 1, 21bl, 44bl, 45tr, 46/47 (main pic), 46tl, 54tl, 56/57 (main pic: lizard), 66/67 (main pic), 68tl, 72/73 (main pic), 84/85 (main pic), 88/89 (main pic). Alex Tomlinson: 40/41 (main pic). Bora Ucack: 10/11 (main pic: clipboard). Clive Watkins: 76/77 (main pic). Neil Webster: 74cl. Darren Wiseman: 86/87 (main pic). ticktock Media image archive: 6bl, 7 (main pic), 12tl, 13bl, 16tl, 17, 21 (main pic), 26bl, 28/29 (main pic), 28tl, 30/31 (main pic), 30bl, 32tl, 42/43(main pic), 42tl, 42bc, 44/45 (main pic),50tl, 53tl, 57bl, 72tl, 74bl, 82bl, 90bl.
With thanks to the Kentucky New Era for providing details of the Sutton story on pages 16-17.

Every effort has been made to trace copyright holders, and we apologise in advance for any omissions. We would be pleased to insert the appropriate acknowledgments in any subsequent edition of this publication.

CONTENTS

ALIENS

IS ANYBODY OUT THERE?

You're driving along a quiet country lane. Suddenly a blinding light flashes in front of you. Your car's engine dies. As you stare into the darkness, shadowy figures creep from the woods. And then... your mind goes blank.

Many people say they have seen or met aliens. Some describe them as small, grey creatures with black, glassy eyes. Others say they look like hairy monsters with sharp, hungry teeth.

Our galaxy contains 100,000 million stars. Scientists believe that other life forms are probably out there, somewhere. But have aliens from outer space really visited Earth? Could they be here already?

Scientists are looking deep into space for signs of alien life. Who knows what they will find? Meanwhile, keep your eyes open. Have you ever woken up feeling that you didn't sleep in your bed last night? And what is that big silver dish doing in your neighbour's garage?

VISITORS FROM OUTER SPACE

Why are aliens here? Some reports are of dangerous aliens kidnapping people, or killing cattle and other animals. Other people describe meeting friendly aliens, such as the movie alien, ET. Are aliens just tourists? Or are they coming to warn us of disaster?

UFOs

How do aliens reach our planet from the other side of the galaxy? Most people think that spaceships, or UFOs (Unidentified Flying Objects), bring them.

Betty and Barney Hill were driving through New Hampshire, USA, in September 1961, when they saw a UFO ahead of them. Then their minds went blank!

Later, Betty described meeting aliens on a spaceship. She had nightmares about them, too. The aliens looked human. They were just over 1.5 metres tall, and had greyish skins and 'wrap-around' eyes.

Betty drew a star map, which she says she saw on a tour of the spaceship. It showed stars in another part of our galaxy. Incredibly, this group of stars was not discovered by astronomers until eight years later!

If UFOs are able to travel through space, we won't be able to follow them very far. The fastest spacecraft made by humans is NASA's *Voyager 1*. But it is thought even *Voyager 1* would take 73,000 years to reach our nearest star (after the Sun).

SURVIVING IN SPACE

So how could aliens survive long journeys in space? Over thousands of years, their bodies would adapt to life in space.

They might find a way to 'freeze' their bodies so they do not get old on long journeys. They could also use robots to explore the universe as we do.

KINDS OF ENCOUNTERS

It's terrifying enough to see an alien spaceship landing. But thousands of people claim they have had contact with aliens or even been kidnapped by them!

In April 1964, policeman Lonnie Zamora was driving along a road in New Mexico, USA. He claimed he saw a silvery spacecraft on four legs. Two strange figures were walking near it. When the figures saw Zamora, they jumped into the craft, and took off with a roar.

A photograph taken by Zamora and his police chief show four prints on the ground from the craft's feet. There were also patches of burnt ground where it took off.

CLOSE ENCOUNTERS – 1 TO 5

Sightings of aliens or their craft are known as close encounters. There are five different types of encounter:

- **Close Encounters of the First Kind** – seeing a UFO within 100 metres or so.

- **Close Encounters of the Second Kind** – finding evidence of UFOs, such as a crop circle or signs of a UFO crash.

- **Close Encounters of the Third Kind** – seeing aliens near a UFO.

- **Close Encounters of the Fourth Kind** – being kidnapped by aliens or being taken on board an alien spacecraft.

- **Close Encounters of the Fifth Kind** – meeting with aliens or making contact with a UFO.

"They were huge round heads... This face had no nostrils... it had a pair of very large dark-coloured eyes, and just beneath this, a kind of fleshy beak. In a group round the mouth were sixteen slender, almost whip-like tentacles, arranged in two bunches of eight each."

A description of the Martians in *The War of the Worlds* (1898) by H. G. Wells.

TYPES OF ALIEN

What do aliens look like? They can look like humans, robots, worms or giant insects. Would you like to meet one of these on a dark night?

Aliens in movies often look like animals. Some have scaly skins, like reptiles. Others behave like insects. They work in gangs to protect an egg-laying alien queen. Watch out for this type, they want to take over the world.

Aliens come in different sizes. Some are huge. Others are so tiny they worm into our bodies, and take them over. Some scientists believe that alien viruses can travel through space. Could they hitch a ride on a comet and crash land on Earth?

ALIEN ABDUCTIONS

In 1957, Villa Boas, a Brazilian farmer, was dragged by aliens on to an egg-shaped spacecraft. Once on board he was stripped and covered in a strange liquid. A blood sample was taken from his chin.

Many people believe they have been taken aboard alien ships against their will. This is called alien abduction. Researchers say the following signs may show that they are telling the truth. Victims usually complain of:

• A UFO sighting.

• Nightmares about aliens; or a nagging feeling that you have met an alien.

• 'Missing time', when you cannot remember where you have been.

• Puzzling scars or burns on your body, and no memory of how they got there.

THE TRAVIS WALTON STORY

In November 1975, seven men who were working in a forest saw a UFO. One of the men, Travis Walton, went to investigate. Walton was paralysed by a beam of light from the UFO. His friends ran away thinking he was dead! Walton's body then disappeared.

Five days later, Walton turned up in a nearby town. Under hypnosis he remembered being kidnapped and examined by three tall aliens with large eyes.

UFO NESTS

Nests are outlines left wherever a UFO has landed.

In 1966, Australian Farmer George Pedley claims he saw a flying saucer lift off from a lagoon. When he went to investigate, he found a large round area of swirling water where the reeds had disappeared.

George went back to the lagoon with a friend. Amazingly, the reeds had grown back. The shape you can see in the picture is the UFO's nest.

ALIEN ATTACK

A famous Close Encounter of the Third Kind took place in August 1955, in Kelly, Kentucky, USA.

Billy Ray Taylor was at the home of his friend Elmer Sutton when a flying saucer landed near the house.

In fear, Taylor and Sutton watched as a little man came towards the house. The alien creature had a big head, long arms with large, clawed hands and huge eyes. The friends shot at the creature. It flipped backwards, and ran off, but the gunshot did not hurt it.

For the next few hours, alien creatures surrounded the Suttons' house. They peered in windows and climbed onto the roof of the house. The terrified family tried shooting the aliens but their bullets could not harm the creatures.

Finally, Taylor and the Suttons ran to their cars, and fled to the local police station.

Afterwards, investigators tried to find evidence of the alien attack, but no sign of them was ever found.

THE ROSWELL CRASH

The disc-shaped object was half-buried in the desert. Around the craft lay four bodies. Their domed, hairless heads had round eyes and slit-like mouths. They were not human...

This famous UFO crash happened in June 1947, outside Roswell, New Mexico, USA. A rancher called William Brazel heard an explosion during a lightning storm. The next day, he found some metal wreckage. The metal was like nothing he had ever seen on Earth. Another local man, Grady Barnett, claimed he had found a crashed UFO and four alien bodies in the same area.

The wreckage was removed by the US Air Force. A few days later, the Air Force reported that the wreckage was from a crashed weather balloon, not an alien spacecraft.

Official reports later said that there had been no UFO and no dead aliens. But many people still believe the truth was covered up.

UFO CRASH SITE

MYSTERY BODIES AT ROSWELL

Some people say that the alien bodies from the crash at Roswell, New Mexico, were taken to a top security storage place called 'Hangar 18' at Wright Patterson Air Force Base, in Ohio, USA.

Others believe the bodies are now stored at Area 51, a secret US government base in Nevada, USA.

Were alien bodies found at Roswell? And if so, where are they now?

ALIEN AUTOPSY

In 1995, an amazing movie was released to the world. The movie had been made in 1947, and showed the body of a dead alien from the Roswell crash.

In the movie, the dead, naked body is lying on a table. It has a large, round belly. Its six fingers are slightly curled. There is a deep cut in its right leg. Its twisted face seems to show pain. Two glassy eyes stare up at the ceiling.

Two doctors stand over the body. They wear white suits to protect themselves from alien infection. First they slice the creature's chest open. They remove its bloody organs. Then they saw its skull in half to look at the brain. On the outside, the creature looks a bit like a human. On the inside, it looked like nothing on Earth.

But did the movie prove that aliens exist, or was it just a hoax?

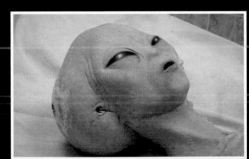

THE TRUTH REVEALED

When the movie was first shown, special effects experts said the alien body was a fake. Medical experts said that the alien's injuries were not from a plane crash. Also, the doctors in the movie did not look carefully at the body. They just dumped the bloody organs into a bucket!

In 2006, the truth came out — the movie was a hoax! An artist had made alien bodies using sheeps' brains and body parts from chickens and pigs.

HOT SPOTS

Where is the best place to find aliens? Some places in the world are UFO 'hot spots'. These are areas where UFO and alien sightings are common.

Brazil has more UFO sightings than anywhere else in the world. In 1980, the town of Tres Coroas was terrorised for 20 days by hovering UFOs.

In Russia, a remote area near the Ural Mountains is known as the M-triangle. Local people in the M-triangle describe strange lights and signs written in the sky. They have also reported meeting glowing aliens in the forest.

If you are worried about aliens, stay away from the east coast of the United States. More alien kidnaps have been reported here than anywhere else in the world!

Aliens aren't fussy about where they land. They've been seen in cities, towns, on farms and even soggy marshes.

NEW YORK ABDUCTION

Linda Napolitano from New York, USA, believed she had been abducted by aliens many times. Under hypnosis she remembered being taken out through the walls of her 12th floor apartment and up to a spaceship. Amazingly, around the same time, two police officers said they saw a woman floating over New York, towards a UFO !

THE CHUPACABRAS – GOAT SUCKERS

This terrifying group of creatures are found mainly in Puerto Rico. Chupacabras are around ¾ metre tall, have huge, red eyes, fangs and long claws. At night they attack farm animals, tearing them apart and eating them.

Some people believe they are the crew of a crashed alien spaceship. Others think they might be escaped creatures from a secret government experiment!

ANCIENT ASTRONAUTS

In the myths of Australian Aborigines, the world was created by spirits called *Wandjina*.

These spirits came to Earth in flying craft from other worlds. *Wandjina* paintings show figures with halos around their heads. Could these halos be the helmets from spacesuits?

ALIENS IN HISTORY

" **M**any large, black globes were seen in the air, moving before the Sun at great speed and turning against each other as if fighting. Some of them became red and fiery and afterwards faded and went out."

This UFO report is over 450 years old! It was written on 7th August 1566, by a student living in Basel, Switzerland. Since ancient times people have reported seeing strange objects and lights in the sky, and mysterious, non-human creatures!

Around 590 BC, the prophet Ezekial took seven days to recover after seeing a "great cloud with brightness around it and fire flashing forth". He also saw four creatures with wings and legs. Could these be ancient aliens?

ALIEN MONUMENTS?

In 1969, Swiss writer Erich von Daniken claimed that alien astronauts had visited Earth. He said that they helped to build the pyramids in Egypt and Stonehenge in England. Most of his theories have now been proved wrong by historians.

ALIEN BOOKS

Many science fiction books and stories have imagined what would happen if humans and aliens met.

One of the first stories about aliens visiting Earth was *Micromegas*. It was written in the 1750s by the French writer Voltaire. Two giants come to Earth from Sirius and Saturn. They laugh at how stupid humans are!

In *The Day of the Triffids* (1951) by John Wyndham, killer plants from outer space take over the world. In Douglas Adams's *The Hitchhiker's Guide to the Galaxy* (1979), Earth is demolished by aliens to make way for a new highway through space!

The War of the Worlds (1898) by H.G. Wells describes a Martian invasion of Earth. After landing in space-cylinders, the Martians build enormous three-legged fighting machines. They destroy everything in their path. Soon red alien weeds cover all of Earth. In the end, the Martians are defeated by a common human germ.

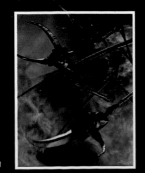

THE FIGHTING MACHINES

"They were described as 'vast spider-like machines, nearly a hundred feet high, capable of the speed of an express train, and able to shoot out a beam of intense heat.'"

A description of the Martian fighting machines in *The War of the Worlds* (1898) by H. G. Wells.

EXPLORING THE UNIVERSE

In movies and TV shows such as *Star Trek* and *Star Wars*, brave human explorers meet strange creatures.

They find many different types of aliens, all over the galaxy. Some of them are intelligent beings, or colourful clouds floating in space. Others are terrifying monsters that gobble up spaceship crews.

MOVIE ALIENS

On their way back to Earth, the crew of a spaceship visit a dead planet. But something is alive there, something terrible...

In *Alien* (1979), a hideous alien life form hitches a ride on a spaceship and gradually kills the crew members one by one. The 'Alien' went on to star in three sequels.

In the movies, aliens love to attack humans! In the very first science fiction movie, *A Trip to the Moon* (1902), exploding moon-men chase astronauts.

Many 1950's movies feature bizarre aliens, such as *The Blob* (1958). In this movie, a meteor carries a giant monster to Earth. It looks like a huge blob of raspberry jam. On Earth, it spreads out and squashes everyone who gets in its way!

IFOS

Thousands of UFOs are reported every year. People get very excited about them because they believe they are a sign that alien life is close by. However, most of the UFO sightings can be explained by weather or man-made objects.

PROJECT BLUE BOOK

In 1947, the United States government began officially researching UFOs. This became known as *Project Blue Book*. Their final report said that there was not enough evidence to carry on the study.

Some people believe that governments try to cover up UFO sightings. They claim that special, top secret agents, known as 'Men in Black', try to stop stories about aliens spreading.

Many UFO sightings are actually man-made IFOs (Identified Flying Objects). IFOs include low-flying planes, balloons and satellites. Sometimes, they are top-secret test planes.

Some IFOs are meteors. Others are clouds with a strange shape (like the one in this picture) which look like flying saucers.

It is very hard to prove a real UFO sighting, especially when pictures are fuzzy or the object appears a long way away. Many UFO photos turn out to be hoaxes or jokes, using models or trick photography.

FREAKS OF NATURE

Natural wonders such as the Aurora Borealis make weird effects in the sky. The Aurora Borealis are lights which can be seen in the sky near the Arctic Circle. They are made by natural electricity in the air.

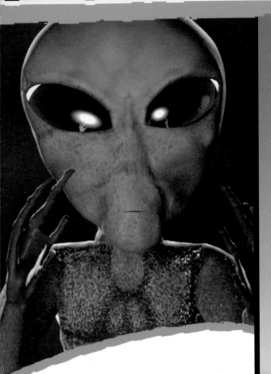

DO ALIENS EXIST?

It is hard to prove whether aliens exist. If aliens are here, they have probably been visiting us for thousands of years already. So don't panic – they haven't harmed us yet!

There may be alien life somewhere in our own solar system. We already know that the planet Venus is too hot and poisonous for life to survive. But in 2004, two robot explorers were sent to Mars where they found signs of water. Where there is water, there is usually life.

Scientists are also looking into space for other planets like our Earth that might be able to grow life. The Hubble Space Telescope has shown that there are billions of galaxies like ours. So there is a very good chance that alien life does exist!

LISTENING FOR ALIENS

Since 1971, scientists have tried to pick up radio signals sent by aliens. So far, no proof of extra terrestrial life has been found.

Scientists from the European Space Agency Darwin project are also looking for planets that could support life. By 2015, they hope to send three space telescopes out into the universe. These telescopes will look for signs of life on other planets.

LIFE ON MARS

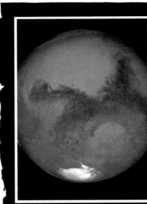

Mars is our nearest planet. NASA scientists believe there is a strong chance that life exists there. They think it's hidden in underground caves. These Martians won't be scary monsters, but tiny microbes.

MONSTERS

WHAT IS A MONSTER?

A great roar echoes around the valley. The ground shakes. Suddenly, a giant shape comes crashing through the trees. Watch out, there's a monster about!

How can you tell if you are looking at a monster? First, look at the size. Most monsters are big. Big enough to swallow you in one bite. Now check out the face. Monsters are ugly, ugly, ugly. Still not sure? Look for huge claws or a mouth full of razor-sharp teeth.

Monsters don't take prisoners. If they don't gobble you up, they'll rip off your head or chew off your arms. Others will toast you with their fiery breath. You have been warned!

If there is a monster living near you, bad luck! Monsters don't die easily. Some have magical powers. If you want to get rid of a monster you'll need to be brave, clever and have superhuman strength!

THE GOOD, THE BAD AND THE UGLY

Don't judge a monster by its looks. Tiny fiends can have evil magical powers. A mighty monster like King Kong can be gentle. An ugly ogre like Shrek can turn out to be a good friend. A beautiful mermaid may lead you to a terrible death.

HERE BE MONSTERS!

On 15th century maps, scary monsters marked unexplored waters. Even today, terrible creatures may be hidden deep in our jungles and oceans.

In the story of King Kong, a movie crew land on mysterious Skull Island in the Indian Ocean. They discover a giant ape, packs of killer dinosaurs and swarms of man-eating insects and slugs.

SHY OR SCARY?

Monsters may be nasty and scary, but they can also be shy. Many avoid towns and cities. Where is the best place to find a monster?

Monsters like to hang out in wild, lonely places such as forests, swamps and moors. These are great places for leaping out on people. No one can hear your screams!

Giant, hairy apes have been spotted on mountains across the world. In Asia, this shy creature is known as the Yeti. In North America it is called Bigfoot or Sasquatch. In September 1967, rancher Roger Patterson filmed a tall, shaggy creature in the mountains of northern California. It looked straight at the camera, then vanished into the woods. Was this Bigfoot?

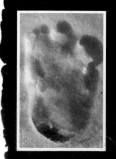

YETI HUNTERS

In September 1951, mountaineer Eric Shipton photographed giant footprints in the snow. Shipton said "where we had to jump crevasses you could see clearly where the creature had dug its toes in." But no Yeti has ever been caught, dead or alive.

MONSTER HUNT

In December 1938, fishermen caught the ugliest fish they had ever seen. It had large, bulging eyes and thick scales. The creature was a coelacanth – a fish that was supposed to have died out 65 million years ago!

Who knows what else is out there? There are still parts of the world where no person has ever been – hidden valleys deep in the jungle, or mountains that can only be reached by helicopter.

Every year, expeditions go in search of monsters like the Yeti or the Loch Ness Monster. Trackers look for unusual marks on the ground. Scientists use hi-tech equipment to search for the creatures underwater or at night.

In 1986, Operation Deepscan used sonar equipment to detect a 73 metre-long shape under the water in Loch Ness, Scotland. Could this be Nessie, the Loch Ness Monster, hiding from the world?

In 2005, an expedition went deep into the Gobi Desert to search for the 'Mongolian Death Worm'. Locals reported seeing a fat, bright red worm about a metre long. They said it spat out a deadly yellow poison!

GIANTS AND LITTLE PEOPLE

Fee Fi Fo Fum. If you hear these words, run! A giant is on its way. Size isn't everything though. Little people can also make your life difficult!

As well as being huge and very strong, giants can be stupid and mean. Their cousins are ogres and trolls. Like giants, they love the taste of human flesh. Luckily, these big bruisers stay at home a lot – counting their piles of treasure.

In the Middle Ages, some people claimed they had dug up the skulls of a cyclops. This ancient giant had one huge eye in the middle of its forehead. The skulls turned out to be elephant skulls, the 'eye socket' was the hole for the elephant's trunk!

A TALL TALE

Giant stories are partly based on famous real-life giants. In the Bible, the future King David kills Goliath. He is a giant warrior, said to be 3 metres tall.

The tallest man in modern times was the American Robert Wadlow. He was 2.7 metres tall when he died in 1940.

LITTLE PEOPLE

All over the world, 'little people' are often blamed when things go wrong. These tiny terrors are known as pixies, goblins, fairies, elves or gremlins.

In the Zulu myths of southern Africa, Abatwa are tiny humans. They can ride on ants! Beware, they are armed with deadly poison arrows.

MIXED-UP MONSTERS!

In 2001, news reports from New Delhi, India, told of a vicious beast. Half-man, half-monkey, it was about 1.2 metres tall. It watched its victims with glowing red eyes and attacked them with metal claws.

Some of the scariest monsters are part-human, part-beast. The Sphinx, which appears in Greek myths, had the head of a woman and the body of a lion. It wouldn't let people pass by, until they had answered a question. It strangled anyone who got the answer wrong.

Centaurs also appeared in ancient myths, and more recently Harry Potter. These fierce creatures had the head and chest of a human, and the body of a horse. Their food was raw flesh.

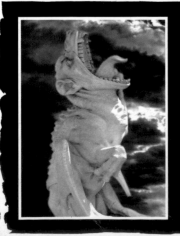

MONSTER FAMILY

Echidna was half woman and half serpent. Her partner was Typhon, a fire-breathing dragon with a hundred heads. Together they made a family of ancient Greek horrors. Among the little darlings were the Chimera, the Hydra, the Sphinx and Cerberus. The worst was probably the Chimera. It was a fire-breathing creature, made up of four different animals.

HUMAN OR MONSTER?

Some monsters can disguise themselves as humans! A bloodsucking vampire can look like you. If you look closely you will be able to spot one. Their pointed fangs are usually a give-away.

FIERCE AND FIERY

"**My** armour is like tenfold shields, my teeth are swords, my claws spears, the shock of my tail a thunderbolt, my wings a hurricane, and my breath death!"

A dragon! This dragon appears in J.R.R. Tolkein's *The Hobbit* (1937). For hundreds of years, people in Europe lived in fear of dragons. These evil, fire-breathing monsters had the claws of a lion, a spiky tail, scaly skin and wings like a bat. But do they really exist?

Dragons seem to look a lot like snakes and crocodiles. The first dragon stories were probably larger-than-life tales about crocodiles and snakes. The Roman historian Pliny described giant lizards living in India that attacked and killed elephants. These were probably crocodiles. In 450 BC, the Greek writer Herodotus described seeing two dragons in Arabia that had been caught and put in an iron cage. Who knows what they really were...

REAL-LIFE DRAGONS?

In 1912 explorers found a giant lizard on an Indonesian island. It was strangely similar to another well-known monster, the dragon. So, they named it the Komodo dragon.

The Komodo can grow up to 3 metres long. Swift and strong, it has poisonous saliva. It can kill a buffalo three times its size by poisoning it.

Komodo dragons have killed over 25 people in the last 70 years.

SKY MONSTERS

Prometheus lay chained to a rock. In the distance he could see a giant eagle. It was coming to rip out his liver. That night, his liver grew again, ready for the eagle's next visit.

MOTHMAN

In November 1966, five men were digging a grave in West Virginia, USA. Suddenly, something that looked like a 'brown human being', with glowing red eyes, flew over them.

Over the next few weeks, there were other sightings of this creature. Some people think it was a Great Horned Owl, shown here. But would you mistake this owl for a human?

This ancient Greek story shows that dragons aren't the only flying terrors. Some of the most deadly monsters attack down from the sky. They snatch up victims in their claws and carry them away.

Harpies are winged monsters with faces like old women. They have long hair and claws made of brass. They punish people who anger the gods by stealing their food. However, anything a harpy touches instantly rots, so harpies always look thin and hungry.

MONSTERS OF THE DEEP

For hundreds of years, sailors have reported attacks by giant squids, slippery sea serpents and other dark monsters. Do they really exist?

"I just saw this grey mass and thrashing tail fin... I didn't see the shark coming as it attacked from underneath. I suddenly felt this enormous pressure, like being gripped in a vice. It wrapped its teeth around the board and my hip, and lifted me out of the water."

An attack by a 3 metre-long Great White Shark, in April 2004, near Port Elizabeth, South Africa. Remember that shark attacks are rare. In fact, falling coconuts kill 15 times more people each year than sharks!

In the 18th century, Dutch captain Jean Magnus Dens was sailing off the coast of West Africa. Two vast arms rose out of the waves. They snatched two of his crew and dragged them under the water. Few believed his story. Then, in the 1940s, a giant squid was measured at 53 metres long!

Few places are as mysterious as the deep ocean. In places it is almost 10 kilometres deep. However, scientists are beginning to explore these cold, dark waters. They use small underwater craft known as submersibles.

In 2002, a mysterious sound, like a giant beast lurking in the ocean depths, was recorded. In March 2006, an eyeless crab-like animal covered in silky blond fur was discovered in the South Pacific. It was over 2 kilometres below the surface.

FROM HUMAN TO MONSTER

Some monsters are born ugly. Others are victims of evil spells or curses. Be careful about who you annoy. You could be next!

In ancient China, people believed their relatives sometimes turned into flesh-eating monsters called Taotie after they died. Taotie had horns and fangs and were half bull, half tiger.

In the Middle Ages, people believed witches could turn themselves into werewolves or vampires. Anyone suspected of being a witch was put on trial. Thousands of innocent people were found guilty and burnt to death.

Many comic book characters are humans with the power to turn into monsters. Spiderman's enemy the 'Lizard' is scientist Curt Connors. After taking a powerful drug, Connors grows into a two-legged reptile. He has tough scales like an alligator, wickedly sharp teeth and claws and the powerful tail of a crocodile.

A BAD HAIR DAY

In Greek myths, if you made the gods angry, you were in trouble! Medusa's mother made a big mistake when she said her daughter looked prettier than the goddess Athena. Athena changed Medusa's hair into snakes and her teeth into tusks. Medusa's tongue turned black and became too large for her mouth, and her hands became bronze claws. If anyone looked at Medusa, they turned into stone.

SCIENCE MONSTERS

The scene: a mad scientist's lab. A huge corpse lies on a slab. Lightning leaps from across the room. It sends a jolt of electricity through the still body. Underneath the sheet, something twitches. The monster is alive!

Monsters can be made when science experiments go wrong. In Mary Shelley's *Frankenstein* (1818), a scientist sews together a monster using parts from dead bodies he has stolen. Then he uses electricity to breath life into the creature.

GENE POWER

Scientists have the power to create new kinds of animals. In the 1990s they created a 'geep', a half-sheep, half-goat mix.

Other scientists have injected mice with jellyfish genes, making them glow bright green.

Not everyone agrees with these experiments. But the new science may help scientists to make new medicines or grow disease-resistant crops.

In R.L. Stevenson's *The Strange Case of Dr. Jekyll and Mr. Hyde* (1886), scientist Dr Jekyll drinks a powerful drug. He turns into Mr Hyde, a monstrous killer.

In *The Hulk* (2003), radiation poisoning turns scientist Bruce Banner into an ugly green giant when he gets angry. Not even the army can stop him when he turns into the Hulk. In the movie *The Fly* (1958), a scientist mixes his genes with those from a fly. He becomes a half-man, half-fly. Like a real fly, he has to be sick over his food before he can eat it!

MONSTER TALES

Over the years, writers have dreamed up all sorts of monsters. If you believe them, blood-sucking vampires, mutants, killer robots and aliens have walked amongst us.

Some of the stranger ones were written about in the Middle Ages. Monks of this age decorated their books with monsters such as the basilisk. This evil creature looked like a cross between a chicken and a serpent!

Many famous monster stories were written in the 19th century, such as *Frankenstein* (1818), *Dracula* (1897) and *The Hunchback of Notre Dame* (1831). Movies are still being made about these monsters. Modern writers such as Stephen King and James Herbert make monsters out of everyday things such as dolls or fog.

"The cruel monster laughed in his murderous mind, thinking how many people now living would die before the day dawned, how he would stuff his stomach with bloody flesh... he suddenly seized a sleeping soldier, slashed at the flesh, bit through bones and lapped up the blood, greedily feasting on giant lumps. Swiftly he swallowed those lifeless limbs, hands and feet whole."

A description of the swamp monster Grendel from *Beowulf*, written around 1000 AD.

MONSTERS EVERYWHERE

In the 20th century, writers created new robot and alien monsters. In John Wyndham's *The Day of the Triffids* (1951) giant flesh-eating plants invade the Earth. Robots take over the world in Karel Capek's play *Rossum's Universal Robots* (1921).

BEWARE THE TRIFFIDS... they grow ...know...walk...talk...stalk...and KILL!

THE DAY OF THE TRIFFIDS

CINEMASCOPE EASTMANCOLOR

HOWARD KEEL NICOLE MAUREY

MOVIE MONSTERS

It is a calm and sunny day. Suddenly, the sea starts to boil. A ginormous lizard rises up. He thumps onshore, crushing buildings and setting them on fire with his fiery breath. Godzilla is in town.

In early movies such as *Frankenstein* (1931), *The Wolf Man* (1941) and *The Mummy* (1942), most monsters were played by an actor in a costume.

In the 1950s, models were used to create giant monsters on screen. Lots of movies were about Godzilla. This monster lizard is woken by an atomic bomb exploding in the Pacific. In *Them!* (1954) giant ants are created by nuclear tests in the deserts of New Mexico, USA. Thousands flee in terror when the ants start to attack.

Today, computers can create amazing monsters on screen. In *King Kong* (2005) a 7.5-metre gorilla fights equally large dinosaurs. Even when you can't see the monster, movies scare you with loud noises and sudden movements.

THEY CAME FROM OUTER SPACE!

Many movies feature monsters from space. In the 1950s and 60s, 'B' movies were made on a small budget. They tried to make scary aliens from bug-eyed turkeys, lobsters and dogs with wigs!

As special effects got better, the monsters became scarier. The *Star Wars* movies are full of weird and wonderful monsters. They come in all shapes, sizes and forms.

NATURAL BORN KILLERS

With an angry screech, T. Rex rushes forward. Jaws open, it crashes into its victim, knocking it over. Huge clawed feet pin down the struggling prey. Razor-sharp teeth tear off giant chunks of flesh.

The *Tyrannosaurus Rex* once roamed all over North America. Luckily for us, it died out 65 million years ago, along with millions of other scary dinosaurs.

A few ancient hunters survive. Crocodiles grow up to 6 metres long. They can kill lions and buffalos. You're also on the menu! Crocodiles wait in shallow waters, then leap out of the water to grab their victim. If their bite doesn't kill you, they'll spin you round and round until you drown.

Deaths and injuries to people from big animals are very rare. Still, there are some scary animals out there. Sharks continue to bite surfers, alligators drag away toddlers, bears maul campers, and tigers attack remote villages.

A DINOSAUR SURVIVOR?

In the swampy jungles of western Africa, many people have reported seeing a strange elephant-sized creature. It has smooth, brownish skin, a long, bendy neck, a very long tail and clawed feet the size of frying pans.

Some scientists believe that this creature, called Mokele-Mbembe by local people, may be a living dinosaur. Since 1980, over 20 expeditions have gone in search of this shy creature, but the beast hasn't turned up – yet!

WHAT ARE MONSTERS?

Good question. Some monsters can be explained as real-life horrors. But what about fire-breathing dragons, giants the size of mountains and other incredible beasts?

In the past, people used myths to explain the world around them. An earthquake was a giant moving under the ground. A whirlpool was a sea monster sucking sailors down. Lightning was two dragons fighting in the sky.

Myths and legends are about real fears. Deadly animal attacks and invading tribes were a constant threat. Warriors wore animal skins to scare their enemies. This is probably where stories about half-human monsters started from.

Modern monsters such as the Yeti may also be real. They are probably not really as scary as we think. The Yeti may just be a large bear or a rare gorilla. Some photographs of monsters are fake, made by people dressed up.

INTO THE UNKNOWN

A few hundred years ago, sailors were afraid of monsters living at the edge of the world. Today, satellites have mapped every part of the planet in great detail. So we worry about them less.

When it comes to outer space, we are not so sure. It's easy to dream up all sorts of strange and terrible aliens! Many look like scary versions of real animals, like spiders, bugs and reptiles.

GHOSTS

INTRODUCTION

WELCOME TO THE SPIRIT WORLD

Tap, tap. In the dead of night, a sound wakes you. Tap, tap. A dark shape appears at the window. Is that a branch blowing in the wind? Or could it be – a ghost!

Be afraid, be very afraid! If you believe the stories, ghosts are all around us. When someone says the word 'ghost', do you imagine a creepy old mansion on a dark, stormy night? Think again. Ghosts can appear anywhere, any time!

Ghosts can walk through walls and even through living people. Ghosts can be a horrible face at the window, a phantom ship floating above the sea or a bright ball of light. Ghosts are said to be restless souls that cannot find peace in death. Some want a proper burial, others want revenge on their killers. If you are lucky, they may ignore you.

Sometimes ghosts do not appear. But they let us know they are there, by moving objects or making strange noises. That icy shudder down your spine could be a ghost walking past…

FRIEND OR FOE?

Ghosts have been giving people goosebumps for centuries. Usually they do not harm the person who sees them. Some good ghosts try to warn strangers of danger. Others attach themselves to children and try to become their friend!

Be warned, however. Some stories tell of less friendly, or evil-minded ghosts. These evil spooks play tricks on people, and push them around. But can we believe such tales? Read on and make up your own mind!

"Ichabod was horror-struck on perceiving that he was headless! But his horror was still more increased on observing that the head, which should have rested on his shoulders, was carried before him on the pommel of his saddle!"

From *The Legend of Sleepy Hollow* (1820) by Washington Irving.

RESTLESS SOULS

What is a ghost? Is it the soul of someone who has died? Or a force of nature we do not understand? Or do ghosts only exist in our minds?

HOLY GHOSTS

Most graveyards are said to have a ghost. In ancient times a living person could be killed to become a graveyard guardian. It was thought that their good spirit would protect the graveyard from evil ones.

The ghosts of priests or nuns haunt churches all over the world. The 'Grey Lady' is a nun who haunts the site of a hospital in York. She fell in love with a young nobleman. When the lovers were found out, the nun was thrown into a windowless room. This was then bricked up to make a living tomb!

NIGHT AND DAY

In Europe, more people claim to see ghosts at Halloween than any other night.

People are afraid of seeing ghosts at night, but most are spotted during the day.

A ghost is often thought to be the spirit, or soul, of a person who has stayed on Earth after death. They might stay to warn a loved one about some danger. Or, they might want to take revenge on a person who harmed them. Ghosts appear all over the world, but people disagree about what they are and how they behave.

In some parts of the world, such as China, people believe that when we die our souls can enter somebody else's body. However, some ghost hunters believe ghosts are just energy left over when people die. So they hunt for ghosts using electrical detectors.

MOORE

LOOKING SPOOKY

Whoooooohh! When you think of a ghost, do you imagine a figure floating around in a white sheet, moaning and dragging clanking chains behind it?

Ghosts do not have solid bodies like living people. People often describe them as being 'silvery' or 'shadowy'. Many ghosts appear in the clothes they wore when they died. In 1953, ghostly Roman soldiers marched through a house in York, England. They wore battle clothes and carried spears. Some ghosts drag chains behind them, a sign that they were criminals.

Many famous ghosts carry their heads under their arm. This is usually because they had their heads cut off. Other headless horsemen ride black horses and carry their heads on their saddles. Some of the spookiest ghosts are those without eyes. When you look at their face, two black sockets stare back at you!

"At this the spirit raised a frightful cry, and shook its chain with such a dismal and appalling noise, that Scrooge held on tight to his chair, to save himself from falling in a swoon."

From *A Christmas Carol* (1843) by Charles Dickens.

HAUNTED HOUSES

It is a wild and stormy night. Lightning flashes and you see a ruined castle in the distance. You need shelter but is this terrible place haunted? Do you dare enter?

Anywhere people have lived can be haunted. This includes inns, schools, theatres and railway stations. Since 1550, a spooky cry has been heard in the streets of Mexico City at midnight. It belongs to the 'wailing woman' who was hanged for murdering her children.

Many old castles have their own ghost. The 'White Lady' walks the battlements of Rochester Castle in Kent. Places where people have been executed are also often haunted. Ghosts at the Tower of London include two murdered princes, and a group of ghostly guards chasing Lady Salisbury – with an axe!

THE MOST HAUNTED HOUSE?

Ghost-hunter Harry Price investigated Borley Rectory in the 1930s. Harry found this mysterious writing on the walls. He also recorded unexplained footsteps, ringing doorbells, smashed glasses, stone throwing and people being thrown from their beds!

The rectory has been called 'the most haunted house in England'. It's easy to understand why!

THE HOUSE OF THE FACES

On 23rd August, 1971, Maria Pereira caught sight of a mark on her kitchen floor. She tried to scrub it off, but it grew bigger. It started to look like a face. The floor was re-laid. Then the face appeared again!

Over the years, different faces appeared and disappeared. Finally the floor was ripped up again. This time workmen found a graveyard. The skeletons were removed and a new floor put down. But the faces kept coming back!

GHOSTLY BEHAVIOUR

WHO'S THERE?

You hear footsteps, see a fork flying through the air and a strange smell fills the room. The hairs on the back of your neck stand up. But, you can't see anything...

We use the word 'ghost' to describe all sorts of strange things that we can't explain. Do you ever feel that something is watching you, even though you can't see it? Or, does part of a room sometimes feel very cold for no reason?

Ghosts get in touch with the living in different ways. They can spook animals, blow out candles or make objects suddenly disappear and reappear again. Some ghosts let us know they are there with strange smells. The ghosts that haunt Cotehele House in Cornwall, England, sometimes fill rooms with a strong smell of herbs!

THINGS THAT GO BUMP IN THE NIGHT

Some ghosts appear to leave behind traces. These can be footprints in the dust, soil or food. Others touch or stroke the living. More annoying ghosts throw objects, move pictures, write on walls and slam doors.

Ghosts also create all kinds of unusual sounds, such as footsteps, knocking, scratching, whispering or bell-ringing. Other ghosts shriek and moan. Banshees are Irish ghosts with a scream so sharp it can shatter glass!

POLTERGEISTS

CRASH! A plate flies across the room and smashes into the wall. You turn around, but no one is there. Then another plate rises into the air. What is happening?

The German word poltergeist means 'noisy ghost'. Poltergeists often attach themselves to a single place or person. Between 1925-27 poltergeists picked on Romanian, Eleonore Zügun, in three different houses. Stones were thrown at her house by invisible powers. Also, strange forces slapped and scratched her face.

A poltergeist likes making mischief and upsetting people. Poltergeists can make objects or even people rise into the air. They also light fires, blow winds through a house, move chairs or slam doors. Having a poltergeist in your house can be a real nuisance, and scary!

THE JOLLER POLTERGEIST

In the 1860s a famous poltergeist pestered the Joller Family. They lived near Lake Lucerne in Switzerland. The poltergeist kept waking them up with knocking noises.

One day the knocking became so loud that the family fled. When the Jollers moved back in, the poltergeist began moving furniture, slamming doors and starting fires.

Another time, an apple mysteriously hopped around the house. A servant threw the apple out of the window, but it came flying back in!

TIDY GHOST

In Russian folklore, a 'domovoy' is a household spirit. It looks like a tiny old man with a face covered in white fur. If you don't look after your home, it tickles you as you sleep, knocks on the wall and throws pans and plates.

GHOSTBUSTING

Do doors slam on their own? Are knocking sounds keeping you awake? Do pictures keep moving by themselves? It's time to call the ghostbusters!

Most people do not believe in ghosts. All the same, large numbers of ghosts are reported every year. Many people take these sightings seriously and investigate them.

The Ghost Club Society of Great Britain was set up in 1862. It was the first organisation to discuss and record ghosts. It also investigates other strange events, known as the 'paranormal'.

Early ghost hunters used candles to pick up ghostly breezes. They also sprinkled chalk or flour on surfaces to find ghostly prints.

Today's ghost hunters use hi-tech equipment. Laptop computers are linked to sensors that start automatic cameras to catch ghosts on video. Sensitive thermometers pick up sudden changes in temperature.

ECTOPLASM

Some ghosts leave behind a horrible sticky mucus called ectoplasm. Ghost hunters say this is what ghosts are made of.

In the early 20th century, ghost hunter and magician Harry Houdini found that most ectoplasm was fake. People blew cotton mixed with goose fat or chewed bits of paper from their mouths. They then called it ectoplasm.

GHOSTS GALORE!

GHOSTLY HABITS

Ghosts have all sorts of unusual habits, just like us! Some ghosts appear just once. Others keep returning to the same place.

The headless ghost of Anne Boleyn haunts eight different places in England. Perhaps she is still angry at her husband King Henry VIII, who had her beheaded in 1536.

GHOSTLY FOLK

A car drives along a road. Suddenly, a hitch-hiker appears at the roadside. The car stops, the hitch-hiker climbs in. Then he vanishes!

Phantom hitch-hikers appear in many ghost stories. Often the ghost asks the driver to give them a lift – to the graveyard where they are buried!

Other ghostly folk include gallows ghosts. In the past, criminals were hung from trees next to crossroads. This is because people thought that if they came back as a ghost, they would be confused by the routes. As a result, the ghost would be unable to leave and haunt them. Their spirits, called gallows ghosts, often appear at crossroads.

Some ghostly folk stay with the same families for hundreds of years. These ghosts may have a favourite bedroom where they sit at the end of the bed! In Denmark, one family ghost looks like a body hanging from a gallows. When the ghost appears, it means someone in the family will die.

GHOSTS OF THE FAMOUS

Many witnesses have reported seeing the ghosts of famous people. Maybe they just want to see a celebrity!

US President Abraham Lincoln was assassinated in 1865. His ghost haunts the White House in Washington, D.C. In the 1930s, Queen Wilhelmina of the Netherlands was staying there. She heard a knock on the door. When she opened it, there stood Lincoln!

GHOSTLY BEINGS

Human ghosts are terrifying enough. Now imagine a ghostly dog, eyes glowing red in the dark, ready to pounce. Watch out for those huge fangs!

Ghost animals are as common as human ghosts. They can be almost any animal you can think of. A ghostly monkey haunts Drumlanrig Castle in Scotland. The ghost of a giant wild horse called the 'White Devil' haunts the deserts of the United States. When it was alive it trampled to death anyone who came near its herd.

The most common ghost animals are black dogs. These often appear to people just before they die. Some of these ghostly hounds have been seen bursting into balls of fire or exploding. Black Shuck is a phantom black hound seen in many parts of England. Arthur Conan Doyle based his famous story, The *Hound of the Baskervilles*, on him.

"Standing over Hugo, and plucking at his throat, there stood a foul thing, a great, black beast, shaped like a hound, yet larger than any hound that ever mortal eye has rested upon. And even as they looked the thing tore the throat out of Hugo Baskerville, on which, as it turned its blazing eyes and dripping jaws upon them, the three shrieked with fear and rode for dear life, still screaming, across the moor."

From *The Hound of the Baskervilles* (1901) by Arthur Conan Doyle.

PHANTOM OBJECTS

Ghostly trains pull into stations where no track remains. Shadowy ships hover in mid-air. These are phantoms, ghostly objects with a life of their own!

"If it is moonlight, clouds cover over the moon as the phantom train goes by. After the pilot passes, the funeral train itself with flags and streamers rushes past. The track seems covered with a black carpet and the coffin is seen in the centre of the car, while all about it in the air and on the train behind are vast numbers of blue-coated men, some with coffins on their backs."

Description of the Phantom Funeral Train in *The Albany Times.*

The ghost of wicked Lady Howard travels in a phantom coach made from the bones of her husbands. The skeleton of a dog runs beside the coach on its journey to Okehampton Castle in Devon. Each night the dog picks a blade of grass to take back to Lady Howard's family home. The coach must take this journey until every blade of grass is picked – that is, forever! It is Lady Howard's punishment for murdering her four husbands.

In 1641, a ship called the *Flying Dutchman* tried to sail around the Cape of Good Hope, in Africa. The ship hit rocks during a fierce storm and began to sink. The captain cried, "I will get around the Cape even if I have to keep sailing until Doomsday". His wish came true! This phantom ship still sails the seas, bringing bad luck to all who see it.

THE GHOSTS OF FLIGHT 401

Worldwide, there are stories of ghost planes soaring silently across the night sky. These ghostly planes seem to turn up after tragic air crashes.

In 1972, an Eastern Airlines jet crashed in the Florida Everglades. Soon after, the ghosts of the captain and engineer saved a plane from crashing by warning the crews of danger.

GHOSTS AROUND THE WORLD

It's a party! Special foods are prepared. Red lanterns are hung. There is dancing and singing. Then fires are lit on the path from the graveyard to the house – to help ghosts find their way to the celebrations!

The Obon Festival described above takes place in Japan each year. After three days of celebrations, floating lanterns are dropped into rivers or the sea to guide ghosts back to the spirit world.

In Mexico, ghosts are welcomed into the home during the Day of the Dead festival. People celebrate the dead with colourful sugar skeletons and skulls. They also have big picnics.

In the past, people in Europe and North America tried to keep ghosts away from their home. In ancient Europe, people believed that Halloween was a night when dead spirits left their graves and wandered the Earth. Today, children celebrate Halloween by dressing up and shouting 'trick or treat'.

THE HUNGRY GHOST FESTIVAL

The Chinese believe the gates of Hell open once a year. Hungry ghosts then wander the Earth looking for food. Families leave out food, so the ghosts will bring them good luck.

They also burn paper models, such as houses, cars, TV sets and mobile phones. They believe that these items will help the ghosts live comfortably in the spirit world. They also burn fake money, called Hell Money, so that ghosts will have more cash to spend!

"Peeves smashed lanterns and snuffed out candles, juggled burning torches over the heads of screaming students, caused neatly stacked piles of parchment to topple into fires or out of windows; flooded the second floor when he pulled off all the taps in the bathrooms, dropped a bag of tarantulas in the middle of the Great Hall during breakfast ....."

A description of Peeves the poltergeist from *Harry Potter and the Order of the Phoenix* (2003) by J. K. Rowling.

SPOOKY TALES

You're sitting around a campfire. It's late at night and someone is telling a spine-chilling ghost story. Then – CRACK! There's a sound in the bushes behind you! Would you go and investigate?

Even people who don't really believe in ghosts enjoy spooky stories. Harry Potter's school, Hogwarts, is haunted by over twenty ghosts, including Nearly Headless Nick, grim Bloody Baron and the jolly Fat Friar. The ghost Myrtle sometimes gets flushed out of the castle with the contents of the toilet! These ghosts enjoy a Deathday Party on the anniversaries of their deaths.

Many other famous books and plays also contain ghosts. They appear in the *Goosebumps* horror series written by R.L. Stine. In *A Christmas Carol* by Charles Dickens, three ghosts visit the miserable Scrooge. They encourage him to be more generous and enjoy life. What's the scariest story you know?

FACT OR FICTION?

MOVIE GHOSTS

A teenager walks along a dusty corridor. The lights flicker. The music gets louder. A ghostly hand reaches out from the darkness. The girl lets out a terrified scream – 'Aaaaaargh!' So does the audience!

Ghost movies have been scaring people for over a hundred years. The first horror movie was *The Haunted Castle* (1896) directed by Georges Méliès. Méliès used trapdoors and mirrors to make his ghosts float and vanish.

Since then, special effects have made spooky faces appear, ghosts walk through walls and poltergeists throw objects. As you can see from this picture, *Ghostbusters* (1984) made the most of these effects.

Some ghost movies are based on stories such as *The Legend of Sleepy Hollow* (1999). Other movies are set in the present. In *The Sixth Sense* (1999), a young boy believes he can see and talk to the spirits of the dead.

GOOD OR BAD SPIRITS?

Some movie ghosts are helpful. Others are mean and try to harm or kill people. There are movies about friendly ghosts, like *Casper* (1995). Casper tries hard to make friends with people, but ends up scaring them.

In the movie *The Frighteners* (1996), the hero gets a bump on his head that lets him talk to ghosts. He joins up with three friendly ghosts to track down killer ghosts.

FACT OR FICTION?

DO GHOSTS EXIST?

After hundreds of years of people seeing ghosts, no one has ever been able to really prove that they exist. What do you think?

Nine out of ten ghosts are probably tricks of our imagination. Tired minds mix up real life and dreams. It's easy to see strange things in the dark.

Terrible events put people into a state of shock. They are more likely to imagine things. For example, an awful tsunami hit the Thai island of Phi Phi in early 2005. Afterwards, many people reported the ghost of a woman calling for her lost child.

Can we trust everyone who sees a ghost? In the past, telling ghost stories was a way of keeping strangers away. Often people claiming to speak to spirits are looking for money or fame. Many are shown to be cheats.

FAKE PHOTOS

Some ghost hunters claim they have taken photographs of ghosts. However, many of these have been proven to be fakes.

In the 19th century, photography was new and most people did not understand how cameras worked. For example, when two shots are taken using the same piece of film, the two images sit on top of each other. This is called double exposure. It makes people look shadowy and ghost-like. Try it yourself with a camera that uses film.

GHOST TOWNS

Quiet places can seem spooky, especially deserted buildings. No one lives in the old mining town of Bodie in California anymore. It is a ghost town. Walking around it feels strange. We expect to see people but we don't.

Water running below a house can cause creaks and groans. At night, houses cool down, making the walls creak. Pipes make gurgling noises. Books fall off the shelves, creating a sliding sound, a short silence, then a giant clatter! Pets make all sorts of night-time noises.

GLOSSARY

Abduction Taking someone away against their will. Another word for kidnap.

Afterlife Where souls travel after death.

Ancestors Members of your family born before you.

Astronomer A scientist who studies space.

Autopsy An examination to find out why someone, or something, died.

Behead To cut off someone's head.

Burial Placing a dead body into a grave.

Cemetery or graveyard. A place where bodies are buried.

Coelacanth A large bony fish thought to have died out millions of years ago.

Corpse A dead body.

Crevasse A deep crack in the ice.

Crop circle A flattened pattern made in a field of crops. Some people believe crop circles are made by people playing tricks. Others think they are made by aliens in UFOs.

Demon An evil spirit or monster.

Detector A machine that finds things.

Ectoplasm The mysterious material that ghosts are supposedly made of. It can be like a mist or a gooey liquid.

Execute To kill someone as punishment.

Expedition A journey taken by people who want to find something.

Extra terrestrial Something from another planet or another part of the universe.

Flying saucer An early name for UFOs. Many UFOs look like big discs or a metal saucer flying through the air.

Foe An enemy.

Galaxy A large group of about 100 billion stars. Earth (which is a planet) is part of the Milky Way Galaxy.

Gallows A large wooden frame used for hanging criminals. It was often built at a crossroads.

Genes A chemical code passed from parents to their young that contains information such as the colour of our eyes or hair.

Ghost town A deserted town.

Haunt A ghost that keeps appearing in the same place is said to haunt that place.

Hoax An attempt to trick people into believing that something false is real.

Hound Another word for a dog, especially a hunting dog.

Hypnosis When a hypnotist uses special words and actions to make someone fall into a sleep-like state. People who are hypnotised can be made to remember things they have forgotten in normal life!

Infect To pass on a disease.

Infra-red Light that is so red we cannot see it. Some cameras use it to make movies in the dark.

Malevolent A malevolent spirit is one that wants to hurt or scare people.

Medium Someone who is sensitive to, and may get messages from, ghosts.

Meteor a piece of rock or metal from outer space.

Microbes Tiny, simple living things.

Monsters Dangerous, scary creatures.

Mucus A sticky, slimy substance.

Mutants Animals or humans whose genes are different. In some stories, mutants have superhuman powers or strength.

NASA (National Aeronautics and Space Administration) An American organisation that studies space and builds spacecraft.

Paranormal This means 'beyond normal'. It describes anything that we can't explain using science.

Phantom A ghostly figure or object, such as a phantom ship or coach.

Poltergeists A noisy ghost that moves things and makes noises.

Robot An electronic machine that moves like a living person or animal.

Radiation Rays of energy. Can be from a nuclear explosion or chemicals.

Satellites Spacecraft that circle the Earth sending and receiving radio and TV signals.

Sighting (UFO/ghost) An occasion when a UFO/ghost has been seen.

Solar system The nine planets, including our Earth, that circle the Sun.

Sonar A machine that uses sound to track objects under the water.

Spook/spectre Other words for ghost.

Spooky Strange or scary.

Submersibles A small underwater craft used for exploring the deep ocean.

Superhuman Having incredible powers or strength much greater than ordinary humans.

Swarm A large group of things.

UFO An Unidentified Flying Object. An object that cannot be explained by human activities or nature.

Universe Everything that exists anywhere!

Viruses Small particles that infect the cells of living things.